T0413982

Horses of Presidents

Grace Hansen

Abdo Kids Junior
is an Imprint of Abdo Kids
abdobooks.com

Abdo

PETS OF PRESIDENTS

Kids

abdobooks.com

Published by Abdo Kids, a division of ABDO, P.O. Box 398166, Minneapolis, Minnesota 55439.
Copyright © 2022 by Abdo Consulting Group, Inc. International copyrights reserved in all countries.
No part of this book may be reproduced in any form without written permission from the publisher.
Abdo Kids Junior™ is a trademark and logo of Abdo Kids.

Printed in the United States of America, North Mankato, Minnesota.

102021

012022

THIS BOOK CONTAINS
RECYCLED MATERIALS

Photo Credits: Alamy, Getty Images, Granger Collection, John F. Kennedy Library and Museum, Library of Congress, Shutterstock

Production Contributors: Teddy Borth, Jennie Forsberg, Grace Hansen

Design Contributors: Candice Keimig, Pakou Moua

Library of Congress Control Number: 2021939926

Publisher's Cataloging-in-Publication Data

Names: Hansen, Grace, author.

Title: Horses of presidents / by Grace Hansen

Description: Minneapolis, Minnesota : Abdo Kids, 2022 | Series: Pets of presidents | Includes online resources and index.

Identifiers: ISBN 9781098209278 (lib. bdg.) | ISBN 9781644946923 (pbk.) | ISBN 9781098209971 (ebook) | ISBN 9781098260330 (Read-to-Me ebook)

Subjects: LCSH: Horses--Juvenile literature. | Pets--Juvenile literature. | Presidents--Juvenile literature. | Presidents' pets--United States--Juvenile literature.

Classification: DDC 973--dc23

Table of Contents

Horses of Presidents

Almost every US president has had pets. Many have had horses!

Washington had many horses.
Nelson and Blueskin were in
the **Revolutionary War**.

6

George
Washington

John Adams was the first president to live in the White House. His carriage horses lived there too!

John
Adams

John Tyler had his horse for 21 years. The horse's name was The General.

John
Tyler

11

Zachary Taylor had a beloved horse. His name was Old Whitey. He **pranced** when music played.

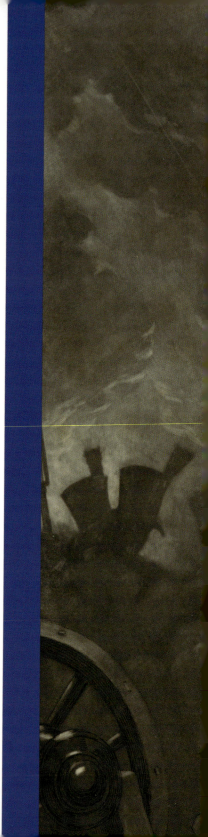

Zachary
Taylor

13

Taylor also got a pony
for his daughter. It was a
former circus pony. Its name
was Apollo!

Mary
Taylor.

Ulysses S. Grant had a favorite horse. He let few people ride Cincinnati. One was Abe Lincoln.

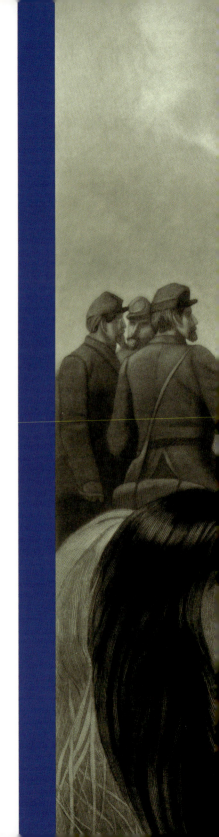

Cincinnati
the horse

17

Teddy Roosevelt had many White House pets. He spent a lot of time with his horse.

18

Bleistein
the horse

The Kennedys had three ponies. The ponies **grazed** the White House lawn.

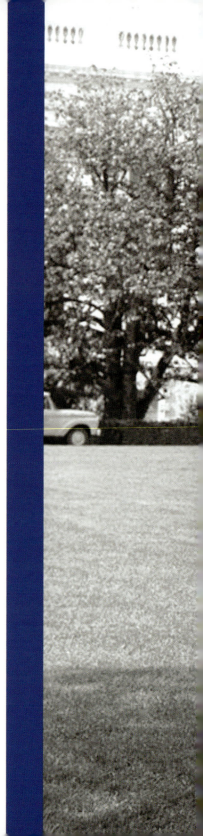

20

John F. Kennedy
and Leprechaun

Caroline Kennedy
and Macaroni

Tex
the pony

21

More First Pets

Andrew Jackson
Sam Patch the white horse

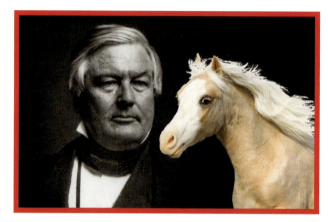

Millard Fillmore
Mason the pony

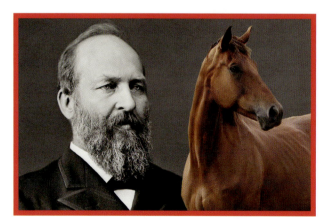

James Garfield
Kit the brown mare

Chester A. Arthur
bay horses

Glossary

graze
to feed on growing grass.

prance
to move with high springy steps.

Revolutionary War
the war of 1775-1783 in which the American colonies won their independence from Great Britain.

Index

Visit **abdokids.com** to access crafts, games, videos, and more!

Use Abdo Kids code

PHK9278

or scan this QR code!